AESOP'S FABLES

AESOP'S FABLES

RETOLD IN VERSE BY
TOM PAXTON

ILLUSTRATED BY
ROBERT RAYEVSKY

MORROW JUNIOR BOOKS/NEW YORK

Library of Congress Cataloging-in-Publication Data
Paxton, Tom.
Aesop's fables.
Summary: A collection of fables from Aesop retold in verse.
1. Fables. [1. Fables] I. Rayevsky, Robert, ill.
II. Aesop's fables. English. III. Title.
PZ8.2.P39   1988   398.2'452 [E]   88-1652
ISBN 0-688-07360-3
ISBN 0-688-07361-1 (lib. bdg.)

AESOP'S FABLES

PATIENCE

A fox was passing through the woods,
As hungry as could be.
He caught a whiff of bread and meat
From deep inside a tree.
"Hold on!" says he. "No tree I know
Would smell like meat and bread.
I think someone has left his lunch
Inside this tree and fled."
And sure enough, inside the tree—
Behind a narrow hole—
Was someone's meal of tasty meat
Wrapped in a crusty roll.
Quick as a wink the fox squeezed in
(Although the hole was narrow)
And Zip! The food shot down his throat
As straight as any arrow.
"Excuse me," fox said to the tree,
"If I do eat and run.
I haven't time to lie about;
I've chores that must be done."
He went to leave the hollow tree,
And thought that would be that.

But what was this? He couldn't leave,
For he had grown too fat!
He tried to squeeze out through the hole
Through which he had squeezed in.
But that was back before his lunch
When he was still quite thin.
Now fox's tummy swelled with meat,
His belly bulged with bread.
The only part that could pass through
Was this poor fox's head.

Another fox was passing by
And heard his mournful cry.
He listened to the fox's tale,
Then smiled and said, "Oh my,
Your problem soon will fade away
If you'll be patient. Then
You'll find that you'll start losing weight
And soon be thin again!
Then, when you're thin, you'll slip right through
Without the slightest pain."
So PATIENCE is the virtue that
We all must strive to gain.

THE FOX
AND THE GRAPES

A hungry fox sat under a tree.

(A very high tree,

Yes, a very high tree.)

And up in the tree there grew a vine.

(A very long vine,

Yes, a very long vine.)

And on that vine there grew some grapes.

(They were juicy grapes,

Yes, the juiciest grapes.)

There were grapes on the vine,

On the vine on the tree,

On the tree where the fox

Sat hungrily licking

His ravenous chops,

Saying, "Dinner at last!

I love the shapes,

The color, the taste,

The smell of grapes.

Yes, grapes are a meal that is sure to please,

And the grapes that I crave the most are *these*—

The grapes on the vine,

On the very long vine,

On the vine on the tree.

Oh, dinner at last!"
Cried the hungry fox
As he danced a dance,
As he spun a spin,
As he tucked a napkin under his chin.
"Dinner at last!" cried the fox as he
Reached for the grapes in the very high tree,
The grapes that hung so temptingly
Just out of reach in the very high tree.
"Oh blast!" cried the fox as he ran and jumped.
"Oh drat!" cried the fox as he groaned and grumped.
For as high as he sprang, and as much as he strained,
Those juicy grapes were not obtained.
The fox might mutter, shout, and screech,
But still those grapes were out of reach.

At last the hungry fox said, "Now
I'll look elsewhere, and anyhow,"
The fox exclaimed with an icy glower,
"I'm certain that those grapes are sour!"

And, like the fox, we rant and rave
When we can't have the things we crave.
Then, like the fox, we're heard to say
We didn't want them anyway.

POOR OLD LION

Poor old lion,
Lyin' in his den.
Never goin' huntin'
In the jungle again.
Poor old lion,
Lyin' there sick.
If you want to see him,
Better see him quick.

Here come the animals,
Payin' a call.
How does he thank 'em?

By eatin' 'em all!
When he's finished,
What's he done?
Eaten his callers,
One by one.

Poor old lion,
Lyin' on some rocks.
Out in the sunlight
Stands Mister Fox.
"Hey, Mister Lion,
You're lookin' mighty thin."
"Yes, Mister Fox.
Won't you step right in?"

"No thanks, Mister Lion.
I'm stayin' right here.
You might feel ill,
But the message is clear.
That you're still a danger,
I have no doubt.
I see tracks goin' in,
But none comin' out!"

THE GOOSE THAT
LAID GOLDEN EGGS

There once was a lucky man
Who lived in days of old.
The gods had blessed him with a goose
Whose eggs were purest gold.
And day by day she laid these eggs
And honked her proud delight.
And day by day these goose eggs shone
With glowing golden light.
And yet this greedy man,
Who watched his fortune grow,
Grew restless with his golden goose
And felt her much too slow.
"You silly goose!" the man complained.
"You must obey your master.
Your golden eggs are welcome here,
But you must lay them faster!"
The goose was glad to try her best,
And eager to obey,
So still she laid her golden eggs—
But only one a day.

At last the foolish man declared
That he could wait no more.
He slew the goose and cut her up
To find the golden store.
He slew the goose to find the gold;
He searched the goose with care.
But to this greedy man's dismay,
He found no treasure there.

The goose was dead, the goose was gone,
The goose was growing cold.
No more this magic goose would lay
Her eggs of gleaming gold.

Alas, this silly, grasping man
The gods had blessed before,
Now lost the plenty that he had
In greed for having more.

GRATITUDE

A lion was dozing in the noonday sun
When a mouse came running as a mouse will run.
He ran over the lion, who awoke with a roar:
"Who's treating my back like the jungle floor?"
He grabbed the poor mouse by his poor little tail.
"Oh, please, Mister Lion, I swear without fail,
If you'll please just release me, I promise someday
The debt will be one that I'll gladly repay."
The proud lion laughed and let the mouse go,
And gave him no thought for a fortnight or so,
Till, captured by hunters and tied to a tree,
He bawled and he bellowed in deep misery.
The mouse (the same mouse he had captured before)
Was passing that way when he heard the lion's roar.
Then quick as a flash to the lion he flew,
And with his sharp teeth the thick ropes he gnawed through.

The proud lion preened and the little mouse pranced,
And there in that glade in the forest they danced.
The little mouse sang, "'Twas the least I could do,
For certainly, sir, I was grateful to you.
Yes, sometimes the weak and sometimes the strong
Must help each other to save right from wrong."

THE TORTOISE
AND THE HARE

"Zip! Zap! Zoom! Look at me go!
I am the hare, and I hope you know
A streak of lightning could not catch me;
I am as fast as fast can be."

"Fast, indeed," the tortoise replied,
"And yet, I wonder, if I tried
To win a race, how well I'd do.
I think I'd like to race with you."

"To race with me is lunacy!
Just search through all of history;
No greater mismatch you'll find there
Than a tortoise racing against a hare."

But the tortoise insisted on racing, and so
The starter cried, "Get ready! Go!"
Then Whiz! Bang! Boom! In a streak of light,
The hare was quickly out of sight.

Zip! Zoom! and Whiz! and Wham! and Screech!
"I guess this race is out of reach,"
The hare exclaimed as he stopped by a tree.
"That tortoise will never catch up with *me*."

He stretched out under the sunny skies,
And very soon had closed his eyes.
He slept and dreamt of carrot pie,
While the tortoise slowly plodded by.

The hare awoke and washed his face,
Then quickly finished up the race,
When—what a shock for Mister Hare!—
He found the tortoise waiting there!

To cheers that rang across the skies,
The tortoise took the winner's prize.
Yes, many there are who race and run,
But slow and steady gets things done.

THE DOG IN THE MANGER

Rowff! Rowff! the brown dog growled.
The brown dog snapped; he snarled and scowled
In a manger filled with hay and oats,
In a stable of horses, cows, and goats.
A horse was there who'd worked all day
While dreaming of nothing but oats and hay,
But now this angry dog said, "No!"
Not one step closer he'd let him go.
"But, sir," the hungry horse exclaimed,
"Surely you must feel ashamed.
Yes, surely shame is what you feel
To keep me from my hard-earned meal.
Why, sir, when you sit down to eat,
I'm certain that you dine on meat;
So tell me why you bar the way
To what *I* crave: my oats and hay."
The brown dog yapped and snapped his jaws
As he dug in the oats with his big front paws.
He said, "Although your words are fine,
You'll get no oats, because they're mine!"

How often, like that selfish dog,
Are we ourselves more like the hog.
Yes, we are selfish when we choose
To keep what we can't even use.

THE WHISPERING BEAR

Two old friends were out for a stroll
When a bear came over a knoll.
One of the friends climbed up a tree.
The other one said, "Bad news for me!"
Then, seeing himself at risk of death,
He lay on the ground and held his breath,
Because he'd often heard it said
That bears will never touch the dead.
And sure enough, the bear walked round
That man who huddled on the ground.
But before the bear left—it did appear—
He whispered something in the man's ear.
When it had gone and they were free,
The one climbed down from the tree.
With clucking tongue and frightened sighs,
He helped the other man to rise.
"The gods be thanked!" he loudly said.
"I thought that you were surely dead.
But tell me: Ere he went away,
What did that ugly creature say?"

"He told me, at the very end,
That I should choose another friend,
Who would not on a troubled day
Desert a friend and run away —
The kind of friend *you* proved to be,
Who ran away and climbed a tree.
So climb your tree; I just don't care—
I hope the next bear finds you there!"

THE BOY
WHO CRIED WOLF

Hey, little shepherd boy,
Fond of your fun,
Crying, "The wolf is here!"
As people run,
Run to assist you—yes,
Run to your aid.
Laugh, silly boy, at
The tricks that you played.
Once, little shepherd boy,
Twice you cried out:
"Help me! The wolf has come!
Help!" you did shout.
Once, little shepherd boy,
Twice people came.
How you did laugh at them,
More to your shame.
Back to their homes they went,
Back down the hill,
While, foolish shepherd boy,
You laughed your fill.

What's this, you foolish lad?
What's this you spy
There in the bushes,
So fearsome of eye,
Tearing among the sheep,
Slaying them all?
"Help, friends! The wolf is here!
Help, friends!" you call.
They hear you calling them—
Women and men—
"Oh, him!" they say. "He
Won't fool us again."
"Help, friends! It's true that
The wild wolf is here!"
Poor, foolish shepherd boy,
Sadly I fear
All of your sheep are lost—
All of them slain;
No gentle sheep will you
Shepherd again.
Please learn your lesson,
Young man, and beware:
Never cry, "Wolf!"
If the wolf isn't there.

THE GRASSHOPPER AND THE ANTS

The grasshopper danced, ta ra, ta ra,
There in the summer sun.
The grasshopper played his violin
And had a world of fun.
The ants, meanwhile, were working hard,
And storing food away;
Puffing and panting day and night,
Laboring night and day.
"Foolish drones!" the grasshopper called,
Turning it into a song.
"Can't you see? There's food enough
To eat the whole day long,
Ta ra," he sang,
"Ta ra," he danced,
"To eat the whole day long."

The grasshopper fiddled his way through June;
He fiddled through July.
He sang and danced all of August away;
September went swiftly by,
Till one cold morning the grasshopper's song
Was heard in the grass no more.
"I don't recall," the grasshopper said,
"Ever being so hungry before.
I say, Mister Ant, it's cold out here,"
The shivering grasshopper said.
He smiled and chirped, "I don't suppose
That you could spare some bread?"
"That's quite correct," the ant replied.
"It's not that we don't care,
But just as you so rightly guessed,
We have no bread to spare.

You laughed at us this summer past,
You called us foolish drones;
But now your songs have died away,
And all we hear are groans.
We worked and saved, we saved and worked,
And now we're snug and warm,
While you may sing and you may dance
All through the winter's storm."

Remember, please, the clever ants:
First we labor; *then* we dance.

97-4